GRAPHIC LIBRARY ®

GRAPHIC SCIENCE

THE EARTH-SHAKING FACTS ABOUT

EARTHQUAKES

WITH MAX AXIOM

SUPER SCIENTIST

by Katherine Krohn

illustrated by Tod Smith and Al Milgrom

Consultant:
Professor Kenneth H. Rubin
Department of Geology and Geophysics
School of Ocean and Earth Science and Technology
University of Hawaii, Honolulu

Capstone
press ®

Mankato, Minnesota

Graphic Library is published by Capstone Press,
151 Good Counsel Drive, P.O. Box 669, Mankato, Minnesota 56002.
www.capstonepress.com

1 2 3 4 5 6 13 12 11 10 09 08

Library of Congress Cataloging-in-Publication Data
Krohn, Katherine E.
   The Earth-shaking facts about earthquakes with Max Axiom, super scientist / by
Katherine Krohn ; illustrated by Tod Smith and Al Milgrom.
   p. cm. — (Graphic library. Graphic science)
   Summary: "In graphic novel format, follows the adventures of Max Axiom as he
explains the science behind earthquakes"— Provided by publisher.
   Includes bibliographical references and index.
   ISBN-13: 978-1-4296-1328-6 (hardcover)
   ISBN-10: 1-4296-1328-9 (hardcover)
   ISBN-13: 978-1-4296-1759-8 (softcover pbk.)
   ISBN-10: 1-4296-1759-4 (softcover pbk.)
   1. Earthquakes — Juvenile literature. I. Smith, Tod, ill. II. Milgrom, Al III. Title. IV.
Series.
QE521.3.K76 2008
551.22 — dc22   2007025091

Art Director and Designer
Bob Lentz

Cover Artist
Tod Smith

Colorist
Krista Ward

Editor
Christine Peterson

Photo illustration credit
Shutterstock/Sean Gladwell, 24 (map)

TABLE OF CONTENTS

To understand what causes earthquakes, we need to know more about the earth.

As you can see, the earth is divided into four main layers.

CRUST

MANTLE

OUTER CORE

INNER CORE

The earth's crust is thin and brittle. Granite and basalt rock make up this layer.

Just below the crust lies a thick layer of hot, flexible rock called the mantle.

Red-hot iron burns in the earth's liquid outer core. The inner core is made of hard iron and nickel.

We live on the earth's crust.

The crust is divided like a jigsaw puzzle into giant pieces called tectonic plates.

But unlike puzzle pieces, tectonic plates don't always fit together.

TECTONIC PLATES

ASTHENOSPHERE

The earth's seven major plates ride on top of the upper layer of the mantle called the asthenosphere.

Seismologists also use the Modified Mercalli Scale to measure how people feel and react to an earthquake. This scale measures a quake's intensity on a scale of 1 to 12.

With a level 1 quake, people don't notice any movement.

A stronger level 6 earthquake will cause trees to shake, and you'll feel the ground move. Cracks will climb up walls, and objects get bounced around.

A level 12 quake is the most deadly and is extremely rare. These powerful quakes cause major destruction and open huge gaps in the earth's crust.

The 1812 earthquakes destroyed nearly half the town of New Madrid, the quake's epicenter. Fortunately, few people lived in the newly settled territory. Only one person died in the disaster.

Another earthquake!

Get outside! The house could collapse on us!

For several days after this devastating quake, the area experienced aftershocks. Aftershocks can occur for days or even years following a large quake.

Earthquakes occur underwater too. On March 27, 1964, a massive earthquake jolted the calm waters of Prince William Sound, off the coast of Alaska. This earthquake had a magnitude of 9.2.

The 1964 Prince William Sound Quake was the largest earthquake ever recorded in North America.

Within 24 hours, several large aftershocks hit the coast of Alaska. Many buildings were destroyed by these aftershocks.

SMITH & MILGROM

When earthquakes happen underwater, they can generate huge waves called tsunamis. The 1964 earthquake created a tsunami that struck the upper west coast of the United States and Canada.

A tsunami isn't just one wave, but a series of waves that travel in all directions across the water. When this wall of water crashes into a shoreline, it can be deadly.

Nearly 90 percent of the earth's earthquakes and volcanoes occur in one main region of the earth.

This horseshoe-shaped region along the Pacific Ocean is called the Ring of Fire.

The area got its name because of the many earthquakes and volcanic eruptions that happen here.

Scientists here in Taiwan and around the world have been researching the Ring of Fire region for years.

They are trying to better predict where and when earthquakes will strike. I'm eager to learn more about their findings.

Unfortunately, people can't always prepare for earthquakes. Old buildings in ancient cities are easy targets.

In 2003, an earthquake with a magnitude of 6.6 rocked the city of Bam, Iran. More than 40,000 people were killed in the quake.

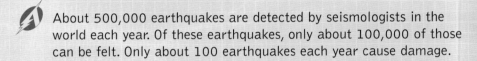

About 500,000 earthquakes are detected by seismologists in the world each year. Of these earthquakes, only about 100,000 of those can be felt. Only about 100 earthquakes each year cause damage.

Scientists have learned that the crustal plate of India collided with the crust of Asia to form the Himalaya Mountains. Scientists believe these mountains are still pushing together and slowly rising.

The largest earthquake of the 20th century occurred in Chile on May 22, 1960. This quake registered 9.5 on the Richter scale. The greatest number of people killed in one earthquake was in China in 1556. The quake killed about 830,000 people.

Tsunami waves can be far-reaching and deadly. Waves from the 1964 Alaska earthquake struck many towns in the Prince William Sound area of Alaska and along the Gulf of Alaska. These waves killed 21 people in Alaska.

Caused by earthquakes, volcanic eruptions, or landslides, tsunamis can travel at speeds up to 600 miles (966 kilometers) per hour.

Researchers in Buffalo, New York, discovered that rubber pads placed under earthquake-resistant buildings can cut the force of a quake by 25 percent.

Geologist A. C. Lawson named the San Andreas Fault in 1895. He named it after the San Andreas Lake, located on the fault, about 20 miles (32 kilometers) south of San Francisco.

 Plate movement along the San Andreas Fault created many mountainous areas. Scientists have studied the Transverse Range segment the most.

 Southern California has about 10,000 earthquakes each year. North Dakota and Florida have had the fewest number of earthquakes in the United States.

MORE ABOUT

SUPER SCIENTIST

Real name: **Maxwell J. Axiom**
Hometown: **Seattle, Washington**
Height: **6' 1"**   Weight: **192 lbs**
Eyes: **Brown**   Hair: **None**

Super capabilities: Super intelligence; able to shrink to the size of an atom; sunglasses give x-ray vision; lab coat allows for travel through time and space.

Origin: Since birth, Max Axiom seemed destined for greatness. His mother, a marine biologist, taught her son about the mysteries of the sea. His father, a nuclear physicist and volunteer park ranger, schooled Max on the wonders of earth and sky.

One day on a wilderness hike, a megacharged lightning bolt struck Max with blinding fury. When he awoke, Max discovered a newfound energy and set out to learn as much about science as possible. He traveled the globe earning degrees in every aspect of the field. Upon his return, he was ready to share his knowledge and new identity with the world. He had become Max Axiom, Super Scientist.

GLOSSARY

continental drift (KON-tuh-nuhn-tuhl DRIFT) — the slow movement of the earth's continents

core (KOR) — the inner part of earth that is made of solid and molten metal

crust (KRUHST) — the outer layer of earth; the crust is made of lighter-weight rocks.

detect (di-TEKT) — to notice or discover something

epicenter (EP-uh-sent-ur) — the point on the earth's surface directly above the place where an earthquake occurs

fault (FAWLT) — a crack in earth's crust where two plates meet

fracture (FRAK-chur) — a break or crack in something

magnitude (MAG-nuh-tood) — a measure of the amount of energy released by an earthquake

mantle (MAN-tuhl) — the layer of hot, dense rock that surrounds earth's core

plate (PLAYT) — a large sheet of rock that is a piece of earth's crust

predict (pri-DIKT) — to say what you think will happen in the future

rupture (ruhp-chur) — to break open or to burst

seismic (SIZE-mik) — something that is caused by or related to an earthquake

seismogram (SIZE-muh-grahm) — the written record of an earthquake

tsunami (tsoo-NAH-mee) — a large, destructive wave caused by an underwater earthquake

volcanic eruption (vol-KAN-ik e-RUHPT-shuhn) — the action of throwing out rock, hot ash, or lava with great force

READ MORE

Armentrout, David, and Patricia Armentrout. *Earthquakes.* Earth's Power. Vero Beach, Fla.: Rourke, 2007.

Burgan, Michael. *The Great San Francisco Earthquake and Fire.* Disasters in History. Mankato, Minn.: Capstone Press, 2008.

Rae, Alison. *Earthquakes and Volcanoes.* Looking at Landscapes. North Mankato, Minn.: Smart Apple Media, 2006.

Simon, Seymour. *Earthquakes.* Washington, D.C.: Smithsonian, 2006.

Thoron, Joe. *Earthquakes.* Kaleidoscope. New York: Marshall Cavendish Benchmark, 2007.

Walker, Niki. *Tsunami Alert!* Disaster Alert! New York: Crabtree, 2006.

INTERNET SITES

FactHound offers a safe, fun way to find Internet sites related to this book. All of the sites on FactHound have been researched by our staff.

Here's how:
1. Visit *www.facthound.com*
2. Choose your grade level.
3. Type in this book ID **1429613289** for age-appropriate sites. You may also browse subjects by clicking on letters, or by clicking on pictures and words.
4. Click on the **Fetch** It button.

FactHound will fetch the best sites for you!